About
Skill Builders
Pre-Algebra

by Tracy Dankberg

Welcome to RBP Books' Skill Builders series. Like our Summer Bridge Activities collection, the Skill Builders series is designed to make learning both fun and rewarding.

Skill Builders Pre-Algebra provides students with focused practice to help them reinforce and develop math skills. Each Skill Builders volume is grade-level appropriate, with clear examples and instructions to guide the lesson. In accordance with NCTM standards, the pre-algebra exercises in this book cover a variety of math skills, including exponents, evaluating and writing algebraic expressions, equations, integers, working with inequalities, fractions and decimals, ratios and proportions, geometry, square roots, graphing, and logical reasoning.

A critical thinking section includes problem-solving exercises to help develop higher order thinking skills.

Learning is more effective when approached with an element of fun and enthusiasm—just as most children approach life. That's why the Skill Builders combine entertaining and academically sound exercises and fun themes to make reviewing basic skills fun and effective, for both you and your budding scholars.

Table of Contents

Powers and Exponents

Part I: Write using exponents.

Example:

$$6 \cdot 6 = \mathbf{6^2}$$

$$x \cdot x \cdot x \cdot x \cdot x = \mathbf{x^5}$$

1. $2 \cdot 2 \cdot 2$

2. $10 \cdot 10 \cdot 10 \cdot 10 \cdot 10 \cdot 10$

= _____

= _____

3. $y \cdot y \cdot y \cdot y$

4. $m \cdot m \cdot m \cdot m \cdot m \cdot m \cdot m$

= _____

= _____

Part II: Evaluate.

Example:

$$3^2 = 3 \cdot 3 = \mathbf{9}$$

$$a^3 \text{ if } a = 2; \ 2 \cdot 2 \cdot 2 = \mathbf{8}$$

5. $9^3 =$ _____

6. $7^4 =$ _____

7. $5^2 =$ _____

8. $10^8 =$ _____

9. m^6 if $m = 2 =$ _____

10. y^3 if $y = 4 =$ _____

Order of Operations

1. $27 \div (6 + 3)$

= _____

2. $9 + 6 \div 3$

= _____

3. $5 + 4 \cdot 7$

= _____

4. $(5 + 4) \cdot 7$

= _____

5. $7 + 6 \cdot 3 - 3$

= _____

6. $15 - (4 \cdot 2) + 8$

= _____

7. $48 \div (32 - 26) \cdot 5$

= _____

8. $6 \cdot 5 - 56 \div 7 + 7 \cdot 2$

= _____

9. $\dfrac{9 + 3}{3 \cdot 2}$

= _____

10. $\dfrac{20 - 8}{9 - 5}$

= _____

Evaluating Algebraic Expressions

Evaluate each expression if a = 2, b = 3, c = 6, and d = 12.

1. abc

$$= \underline{\ 2 \times 3 \times 6 = 36\ }$$

2. $(a + d) - (b + c)$

$$= \underline{\hspace{3cm}}$$

3. $\dfrac{d}{a}$

$$= \underline{\hspace{3cm}}$$

4. b^2

$$= \underline{\hspace{3cm}}$$

5. $\dfrac{c}{a} + 2b$

$$= \underline{\hspace{3cm}}$$

6. $3a^2 - d$

$$= \underline{\hspace{3cm}}$$

7. $cd - ab$

$$= \underline{\hspace{3cm}}$$

8. $bc - d$

$$= \underline{\hspace{3cm}}$$

9. $3d + a^2 - b$

$$= \underline{\hspace{3cm}}$$

10. $\dfrac{bc}{a} + d$

$$= \underline{\hspace{3cm}}$$

Solving Equations Using Addition and Subtraction

Solve each equation.

1. $n + 28 = 84$

$n = $ _____

2. $x - 48 = 129$

$x = $ _____

3. $y + 59 = 194$

$y = $ _____

4. $b + 48 = 190$

$b = $ _____

5. $p - 167 = 75$

$p = $ _____

6. $r - 46 = 278$

$r = $ _____

7. $x + 87 = 364$

$x = $ _____

8. $a - 76 = 695$

$a = $ _____

Solve each equation.

1. $x - 41 = 19$

x = _____

2. $b + 63 = 209$

b = _____

3. $111 = w + 47$

w = _____

4. $y - 87 = 409$

y = _____

5. $k + 283 = 391$

k = _____

6. $r - 116 = 394$

r = _____

7. $x - 365 = 52$

x = _____

8. $83 = p + 52$

p = _____

9. $211 = x + 19$

x = _____

10. $m - 57 = 54$

m = _____

Solving Equations Using Multiplication and Division

Solve each equation.

Example:

$$8x = 192$$
$$\frac{8x}{8} = \frac{192}{8}$$
$$x = \mathbf{24}$$

$$\frac{y}{5} = 26$$
$$\frac{y}{5} \cdot 5 = 26 \cdot 5$$
$$y = \mathbf{130}$$

1. $2y = 98$

y = _____

2. $7x = 168$

x = _____

3. $\frac{b}{22} = 6$

b = _____

4. $\frac{x}{23} = 9$

x = _____

5. $33 = \frac{y}{16}$

y = _____

6. $27m = 972$

m = _____

7. $432 = 36a$

a = _____

8. $84 = \frac{m}{47}$

m = _____

Solve each equation.

1. $9m = 207$

$m =$ _____

2. $\dfrac{x}{37} = 14$

$x =$ _____

3. $475 = 19a$

$a =$ _____

4. $23k = 276$

$k =$ _____

5. $\dfrac{b}{4} = 404$

$b =$ _____

6. $24 = \dfrac{r}{30}$

$r =$ _____

7. $18p = 486$

$p =$ _____

8. $\dfrac{x}{54} = 11$

$x =$ _____

9. $288 = 16w$

$w =$ _____

10. $16 = \dfrac{n}{31}$

$n =$ _____

Integers

Part I: Give the integer for each number on the number line.

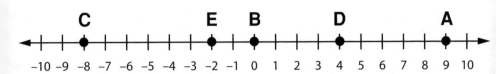

1. A = _____   **2.** B = _____   **3.** C = _____   **4.** D = _____   **5.** E = _____

Part II: Give the absolute value.

Absolute value is the distance a number is from zero and is denoted by two straight lines around the number. For example, the absolute value of |⁻4| is 4 because ⁻4 is 4 places from zero.

6. |⁻2| = _____

7. |8| = _____

8. |⁻5| = _____

9. |12| = _____

10. |⁻21| = _____

11. |⁻83| = _____

12. |100| = _____

13. |⁻142| = _____

14. |⁻231| = _____

15. |250| = _____

Comparing and Ordering Integers

Part I: Use <, >, or = for each ◯.

1. ⁻8 ◯ 8   **2.** 0 ◯ ⁻3

3. 15 ◯ ⁻16   **4.** |⁻4| ◯ 4

5. ⁻12 ◯ ⁻20   **6.** ⁻3 ◯ |⁻4|

Part II: Put the integers in order from least to greatest.

7. ⁻4, ⁻2, 5   **8.** ⁻2, ⁻7, ⁻10, ⁻3

= _____   = _____

9. ⁻14, 12, |⁻17|, 5   **10.** ⁻3, |⁻4|, ⁻2, |5|

= _____   = _____

Adding Integers

Find each sum.

Adding Like Integers
1. Add their absolute values.
2. Use the sign of both numbers.

$-8 + (-20) = -28$; $|-8| + |-20| = 28$

Since both numbers are negative, the sum is negative.

$$-8 + (-20) = \mathbf{-28}$$

Adding Unlike Integers
1. Subtract their absolute values.
2. Use the sign of the greater
absolute value.

$$-10 + 8 = -2$$
$$|-10| = 10 \quad |8| = 8$$
$$10 - 8 = 2$$
$$|-10| > |8|$$

So, the answer is **-2**.

1. $8 + (-18)$

= _____

2. $-7 + (-8)$

= _____

3. $-8 + 24$

= _____

4. $-9 + (-3)$

= _____

5. $26 + 8$

= _____

6. $-24 + 0$

= _____

Subtracting Integers

Find each difference.

1. $4 - 10 = $ _____

2. $^-5 - 12 = $ _____

3. $3 - (^-15) = $ _____

4. $^-7 - (^-14) = $ _____

5. $8 - 14 = $ _____

6. $34 - (^-10) = $ _____

7. $^-22 - (^-38) = $ _____

8. $6 - 15 = $ _____

9. $^-54 - 94 = $ _____

10. $7 - (^-7) = $ _____

11. $^-7 - 7 = $ _____

12. $^-7 - (^-7) = $ _____

Solving Integer Equations Using Addition and Subtraction

Solve each equation.

1. $c - 15 = {}^-10$

$c = $ _____

2. $a + 57 = {}^-60$

$a = $ _____

3. $b + 58 = {}^-110$

$b = $ _____

4. $y - 28 = {}^-28$

$y = $ _____

5. $42 = p + ({}^-25)$

$p = $ _____

6. ${}^-37 = x + 85$

$x = $ _____

7. $y - ({}^-12) = 49$

$y = $ _____

8. $r - 62 = {}^-341$

$r = $ _____

9. ${}^-317 = y - 97$

$y = $ _____

10. $132 = c - ({}^-249)$

$c = $ _____

Multiplying Integers

Find each product.

1. $5(-9) =$ _____

2. $-6(-7) =$ _____

3. $-7(3) =$ _____

4. $5(6) =$ _____

5. $-6(-5) =$ _____

6. $-9(9) =$ _____

7. $-8(0) =$ _____

8. $8(-9) =$ _____

9. $-12(12) =$ _____

10. $-10(-46) =$ _____

11. $8(-5) =$ _____

12. $-12(-8) =$ _____

Dividing Integers

Find each quotient.

1. $-20 \div (^-5) =$ _____

2. $81 \div 9 =$ _____

3. $-48 \div 8 =$ _____

4. $30 \div (^-5) =$ _____

5. $0 \div (^-12) =$ _____

6. $42 \div (^-6) =$ _____

7. $\dfrac{125}{^-5} =$ _____

8. $\dfrac{^-96}{12} =$ _____

9. $-90 \div (^-10) =$ _____

10. $-54 \div 3 =$ _____

11. $-75 \div (^-15) =$ _____

12. $52 \div (^-4) =$ _____

Solving Integer Equations Using Multiplication and Division

Solve each equation.

1. $2x = {}^-86$

x = _____

2. $^-4y = 112$

y = _____

3. $\dfrac{b}{^-26} = 7$

b = _____

4. $\dfrac{x}{^-36} = 11$

x = _____

5. $^-8c = {}^-272$

c = _____

6. $105 = {}^-7n$

n = _____

7. $^-x = 45$

x = _____

8. $^-32 = {}^-m$

m = _____

9. $\dfrac{y}{^-8} = {}^-265$

y = _____

10. $^-43 = \dfrac{x}{16}$

x = _____

Solving Inequalities Using Addition and Subtraction

Solve each inequality.

Solve inequalities using addition and subtraction just like you would solve equations.

$$x - 2 < {}^-14$$
$$x - 2 + 2 < {}^-14 + 2$$
$$x < {}^-\mathbf{12}$$

$$y + ({}^-8) \geq {}^-6$$
$$y + ({}^-8) - ({}^-8) \geq {}^-6 - ({}^-8)$$
$$y \geq \mathbf{2}$$

1. $m + 13 > 8$

2. $y - 7 < 10$

_____

_____

3. $p - 12 \leq {}^-6$

4. $11 + m \geq {}^-39$

_____

_____

5. $4 < y - 33$

6. $10 \geq m - ({}^-2)$

_____

_____

7. $p - 7 \geq {}^-31$

8. $^-67 + x \geq {}^-28$

_____

_____

Solving Inequalities Using Multiplication and Division

Solve each inequality.

> Solve inequalities using multiplication and division like you would solve equations; *however*, when multiplying or dividing by a negative integer, reverse the order symbol ($<$, $>$, $\leq$, $\geq$).
>
> $$-3x \leq 21$$
> $$\frac{-3x}{-3} \geq \frac{21}{-3}$$
> $$x \geq \mathbf{-7}$$
>
> $$\frac{p}{6} \leq -12$$
> $$\frac{p}{6}(6) \leq -12(6)$$
> $$p \leq \mathbf{-72}$$

1. $\dfrac{m}{-8} > 21$

2. $-3n \leq 51$

_____

_____

3. $11y > {}^-121$

4. $\dfrac{x}{-9} \geq 7$

_____

_____

5. $25 < 5n$

6. $-12x > 48$

_____

_____

7. $-6n \geq -36$

8. $\dfrac{w}{3} < 28$

_____

_____

Adding and Subtracting with Decimals

Find each sum or difference.

Example:

Line the decimals up, writing the numbers vertically; then add or subtract.

$$11.83 + 12.81 + 12.93 + 11.12 =$$

$$
\begin{array}{r}
\overset{2}{1}1.83 \\
12.81 \\
12.93 \\
+\ 11.12 \\
\hline
\mathbf{48.69}
\end{array}
$$

1. $93.3 - 24.6$

= _____

2. $8.6 + 59.2$

= _____

3. $6.8 + 21.3 + 42$

= _____

4. $8.083 - 4.681$

= _____

5. $2.81 + 9.63 - 2.7$

= _____

6. $5.98 + 0.09 + 0.62$

= _____

7. $68.14 - (^-32.48)$

= _____

8. $7.92 + (^-2.67)$

= _____

Solving Decimal Equations Using Addition and Subtraction

Solve each equation.

Example:

$$x + 0.31 = 6.22$$
$$x + 0.31 - 0.31 = 6.22 - 0.31$$
$$x = \mathbf{5.91}$$

1. $y - 1.78 = 3.6$

$y =$ _____

2. $y + 19.3 = 21$

$y =$ _____

3. $p + 0.243 = {}^-3.6$

$p =$ _____

4. $x - 2.34 = 6.8$

$x =$ _____

5. $m + 1.52 = {}^-36.61$

$m =$ _____

6. $a - 5.05 = {}^-3.38$

$a =$ _____

7. $28.05 + b = 92.5$

$b =$ _____

8. $w - 32.7 = {}^-6.41$

$w =$ _____

Multiplying with Decimals

Find each product.

$2.03 \times (^-0.2) = ^-0.406$

$$
\begin{array}{r}
2.03 \\
\times\ -0.2 \\
\hline
^-.406
\end{array}
\left.\begin{array}{l} \\ \\ \\ \end{array}\right\}
\begin{array}{l}
\text{2 decimal places} \\
\text{1 decimal places} \\
\text{3 decimal places}
\end{array}
$$

1. 19.8×0.01

= _____

2. $5.02 \times (^-0.33)$

= _____

3. $^-33.5 \times (^-0.1)$

= _____

4. $^-5.38 \times 0.08$

= _____

5. $5{,}280 \times (^-0.01)$

= _____

6. 15.32×2.03

= _____

7. $^-39.6 \times 20.3$

= _____

8. $75.2 \times (^-100)$

= _____

Dividing with Decimals

Find each quotient.

Example:

$$17.25 \div 1.5 = 11.5$$

$$
\begin{array}{r}
11.5 \\
1.5{\overline{\smash{\big)}\,17.2\,5}} \\
\underline{-15} \\
22 \\
\underline{-15} \\
75 \\
\underline{-75} \\
0
\end{array}
$$

1. $0.0483 \div (^-2.1)$

= _____

2. $1.6758 \div 21$

= _____

3. $^-51.3 \div (^-1.9)$

= _____

4. $109.5 \div (^-0.05)$

= _____

5. $^-10.4 \div 0.02$

= _____

6. $0.0045 \div 1.8$

= _____

7. $^-0.0315 \div (^-0.7)$

= _____

8. $131.58 \div (^-8.6)$

= _____

Solving Decimal Equations Using Multiplication and Division

Solve each equation.

Example:

$$\frac{x}{0.14} = 5.2$$

$$\frac{x}{0.14}(0.14) = 5.2(0.14)$$

$$x = \mathbf{0.728}$$

$$^-1.5x = 225$$

$$\frac{^-1.5x}{^-1.5} = \frac{225}{^-1.5}$$

$$x = ^-\mathbf{150}$$

1. $0.15y = ^-0.24$

2. $^-4.5m = 67.5$

y = _____

m = _____

3. $\frac{p}{^-1.2} = ^-0.91$

4. $3.2 = \frac{x}{^-5.4}$

p = _____

x = _____

5. $^-1.005y = ^-20.1$

6. $3.6r = ^-43.2$

y = _____

r = _____

7. $\frac{^-x}{0.55} = 0.2$

8. $\frac{m}{^-4.98} = 1.2$

x = _____

m = _____

Reducing Fractions

Write each fraction in lowest terms.

Example:

$$\frac{24}{36} = \frac{24 \div 12}{36 \div 12} = \frac{2}{3}$$

1. $\frac{12}{20}$

2. $\frac{7}{12}$

3. $\frac{70}{105}$

= _____

= _____

= _____

4. $\frac{21}{35}$

5. $\frac{63}{81}$

6. $\frac{88}{121}$

= _____

= _____

= _____

7. $\frac{78}{112}$

8. $\frac{14}{56}$

9. $\frac{105}{126}$

= _____

= _____

= _____

10. $\frac{66}{102}$

11. $\frac{15ab}{48b}$

12. $\frac{abc}{2bc}$

= _____

= _____

= _____

Improper Fractions and Mixed Numbers

Part I: Write each improper fraction as an integer or mixed number in lowest terms.

1. $\frac{25}{6}$

2. $\frac{54}{3}$

3. $\frac{338}{10}$

= _____

= _____

= _____

4. $\frac{230}{35}$

5. $\frac{75}{12}$

6. $\frac{80}{16}$

= _____

= _____

= _____

Part II: Write each mixed number as an improper fraction in lowest terms.

Example:

$$5\frac{7}{9} = \frac{52}{9} \qquad 5 \times 9 + 7 = \mathbf{52}$$

7. $2\frac{9}{16}$

8. $6\frac{7}{11}$

9. $8\frac{9}{30}$

= _____

= _____

= _____

10. $10\frac{9}{10}$

11. $5\frac{3}{50}$

12. $20\frac{7}{8}$

= _____

= _____

= _____

Comparing and Ordering Fractions

Part I: Use <, >, or = for each ◯.

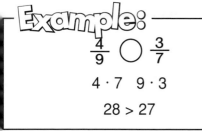

Example:

$$\frac{4}{9} \bigcirc \frac{3}{7}$$

$$4 \cdot 7 \quad 9 \cdot 3$$

$$28 > 27$$

$$\frac{4}{9} \;\bigcirc\!\!\!> \frac{3}{7}$$

1. $\frac{5}{6} \bigcirc \frac{4}{7}$

2. $\frac{9}{13} \bigcirc \frac{8}{15}$

3. $\frac{9}{24} \bigcirc \frac{2}{5}$

4. $\frac{14}{25} \bigcirc \frac{16}{30}$

Part II: Write in order from least to greatest.

5. $\frac{2}{5}, \frac{2}{3}, \frac{2}{4}$

6. $\frac{6}{7}, \frac{7}{8}, \frac{3}{8}$

= _____

= _____

7. $\frac{-3}{4}, \frac{-7}{8}, \frac{-5}{9}$

8. $\frac{-5}{13}, \frac{-6}{15}, \frac{-2}{3}$

= _____

= _____

Adding and Subtracting Fractions with Like Denominators

Find each sum or difference. Reduce to lowest terms.

1. $\frac{9}{13} - \frac{3}{13}$

2. $\frac{5}{11} + \frac{2}{11}$

= _____

= _____

3. $\frac{7}{18} - \frac{11}{18}$

4. $\frac{12}{7} + \left(\frac{-11}{7}\right)$

= _____

= _____

5. $\frac{-2}{15} + \frac{13}{15}$

6. $\frac{3}{16} - \frac{5}{16}$

= _____

= _____

7. $\frac{-9}{10} - \left(\frac{-9}{10}\right)$

8. $\frac{-25}{14} + \left(\frac{-13}{14}\right)$

= _____

= _____

Adding and Subtracting Fractions with Unlike Denominators

Find each sum or difference. Reduce to lowest terms.

1. $\frac{4}{5} + \frac{7}{25}$

= _____

2. $\frac{5}{6} - \frac{3}{4}$

= _____

3. $\frac{3}{4} - \frac{1}{5}$

= _____

4. $\frac{5}{6} + \frac{7}{10}$

= _____

5. $\frac{3}{4} - \frac{4}{7}$

= _____

6. $\frac{^-2}{5} - \frac{3}{4}$

= _____

7. $\frac{5}{18} - \left(\frac{^-3}{6}\right)$

= _____

8. $\frac{^-3}{10} + \frac{6}{15}$

= _____

27

Adding and Subtracting Mixed Numbers

Find each sum or difference. Reduce to lowest terms.

Example:

$$1\frac{1}{2} + 2\frac{3}{4} = 4\frac{1}{4} \longrightarrow \frac{3}{2} + \frac{11}{4} = \frac{6}{4} + \frac{11}{4} = \frac{17}{4} = 4\frac{1}{4}$$

---

1. $5\frac{3}{4} + 6\frac{1}{3}$

    = _____

2. $4\frac{5}{12} - 3\frac{2}{3}$

    = _____

3. $^-4\frac{3}{10} + 7\frac{3}{4}$

    = _____

4. $^-4 - 2\frac{4}{7}$

    = _____

5. $3\frac{3}{5} - \frac{2}{3}$

    = _____

6. $3\frac{5}{9} - \left(^-3\frac{2}{5}\right)$

    = _____

7. $4\frac{1}{3} - 1\frac{1}{3}$

    = _____

8. $\frac{^-3}{7} + 1\frac{3}{7}$

    = _____

Solving Equations Using Addition and Subtraction

Solve each equation. Reduce to lowest terms.

1. $x - \frac{2}{3} = \frac{4}{9}$

x = _____

2. $a + \left(\frac{-2}{3}\right) = {}^-6$

a = _____

3. $m + \frac{3}{8} = 2\frac{1}{2}$

m = _____

4. $x - 2\frac{1}{8} = 3\frac{3}{8}$

x = _____

5. $b + \left(\frac{-3}{20}\right) = \frac{-2}{5}$

b = _____

6. $\frac{6}{5} = \frac{2}{3} + n$

n = _____

7. $x - \frac{3}{10} = \frac{-2}{50}$

x = _____

8. $\frac{9}{16} + y = \frac{-13}{15}$

y = _____

Multiplying Fractions

Find each product. Reduce to lowest terms.

$$2\frac{2}{5}\left(1\frac{5}{12}\right) = 3\frac{2}{5} \longrightarrow \frac{\overset{1}{\cancel{12}}}{5} \cdot \frac{17}{\underset{1}{\cancel{12}}} = \frac{17}{5} = 3\frac{2}{5}$$

1. $\frac{7}{8}\left(\frac{1}{2}\right)$

= _____

2. $\frac{\text{-}5}{6}\left(\frac{2}{5}\right)$

= _____

3. $8\frac{1}{3}\left(\text{-}2\frac{2}{5}\right)$

= _____

4. $\text{-}5\left(\frac{3}{5}\right)$

= _____

5. $9\frac{3}{5}\left(\frac{5}{12}\right)$

= _____

6. $\text{-}4\frac{5}{6}\left(2\frac{2}{3}\right)$

= _____

7. $\text{-}2\frac{3}{4}\left(\text{-}2\frac{1}{2}\right)$

= _____

8. $8\left(5\frac{2}{5}\right)$

= _____

Dividing Fractions

Find each quotient. Reduce to lowest terms.

$$1\frac{3}{4} \div 2\frac{1}{2} = \frac{7}{10} \longrightarrow \frac{7}{4} \div \frac{5}{2} = \frac{7}{\underset{2}{4}} \cdot \frac{\overset{1}{2}}{5} = \frac{7}{10}$$

1. $\frac{5}{8} \div \frac{7}{8}$

= _____

2. $\frac{9}{12} \div \frac{5}{6}$

= _____

3. $\frac{-3}{8} \div 5$

= _____

4. $^{-}10 \div \frac{5}{2}$

= _____

5. $6\frac{1}{8} \div 4\frac{2}{3}$

= _____

6. $2\frac{3}{5} \div \left(-3\frac{6}{7}\right)$

= _____

7. $^{-}6\frac{1}{4} \div 10\frac{1}{4}$

= _____

8. $^{-}2\frac{1}{2} \div \left(1\frac{3}{4}\right)$

= _____

Solving Equations Using Multiplication and Division

Solve each equation. Reduce to lowest terms.

Example:

$$\frac{3}{4}y = \frac{5}{8}$$

$$\frac{4}{3}\left(\frac{3}{4}y\right) = \frac{5}{8}\left(\frac{4}{3}\right)$$

$$y = \frac{5}{6}$$

1. $6m = \frac{3}{8}$

m = _____

2. $\frac{x}{7} = \frac{4}{5}$

x = _____

3. $\frac{-1}{2}x = \frac{7}{10}$

x = _____

4. $1\frac{2}{3}x = \frac{6}{5}$

x = _____

5. $\frac{-3}{5}p = \frac{2}{3}$

p = _____

6. $\frac{5}{8}y = 4$

y = _____

7. $4\frac{3}{5}y = {}^-8$

y = _____

8. $\frac{x}{12} = 2\frac{3}{10}$

x = _____

More Exponents

Simplify. Write each expression with exponents.

1. $\dfrac{2^6}{2^5}$

= _____

2. $\dfrac{9^5}{9}$

= _____

3. $\dfrac{(^-3)^7}{(^-3)^5}$

= _____

4. $\dfrac{5^2}{5}$

= _____

5. $\dfrac{m^6}{m^4}$

= _____

6. $\dfrac{x^7}{x^2}$

= _____

7. $\dfrac{(^-4)^4}{(^-4)}$

= _____

8. $\dfrac{y^7}{y^4}$

= _____

Solving Two-Step Equations

Solve each equation.

Example:

$$6x + 36 = 144$$
$$6x + 36 - 36 = 144 - 36$$
$$\frac{6x}{6} = \frac{108}{6}$$
$$x = \mathbf{18}$$

1. $7y - 13 = 50$

y = _____

2. $5x + 43 = 68$

x = _____

3. $3p - 6 = 9$

p = _____

4. $0.8c + 3.4 = 7.2$

c = _____

5. $\dfrac{m + 4}{6} = {}^-4$

m = _____

6. $\dfrac{x}{8} + 10 = 13$

x = _____

7. $49 = 7(y - 7)$

y = _____

8. $3p + 5 = {}^-37$

p = _____

Variables on Both Sides

Solve each equation.

$$4x + 12 = 6x$$
$$4x - 4x + 12 = 6x - 4x$$
$$\frac{12}{2} = \frac{2x}{2}$$
$$6 = x \text{ or } x = 6$$

You want to get the variables on one side and numbers on the other.

1. $28 + x = 8x$

x = _____

2. $7p = 15 + 2p$

p = _____

3. $3y = 36 + 9y$

y = _____

4. $6m = {}^-6m + 144$

m = _____

5. $4a - 8 = 9a + 7$

a = _____

6. $^-5y - 9 = 3y + 15$

y = _____

7. $18 + 2x = 11x$

x = _____

8. $5y = 30 - y$

y = _____

Solving Multi-Step Equations

Solve each equation.

Example:

$$6 + 3(y + 1) = 4y + 10$$
$$6 + 3y + 3 = 4y + 10 \quad \longleftarrow \text{Distributive property}$$
$$9 + 3y = 4y + 10 \quad \longleftarrow \text{Combine like terms.}$$
$$9 + 3y - 3y = 4y - 3y + 10 \quad \longleftarrow \text{Subtract 3y from both sides.}$$
$$9 = y + 10$$
$$9 - 10 = y + 10 - 10 \quad \longleftarrow \text{Subtract 10 from both sides.}$$
$$^-1 = y \text{ or } y = {}^-1$$

1. $2(c - 3) + 5 = 3c - 3$

2. $4x + 20 = 2x + 12$

c = _____

x = _____

3. $\frac{4}{7}p - 6 = \frac{2}{7}p + 12$

4. $^-10 + 7(a + 3) = 4(2a - 1) + 5$

p = _____

a = _____

More Practice

Solve each equation.

1. $19x - 13x = 12$

x = _____

2. $15y = 3(y + 8)$

y = _____

3. $\dfrac{a + 8}{4} = 20$

a = _____

4. $7p + 8 = 3p - 12$

p = _____

5. $\dfrac{7}{9}y + 2 = \dfrac{5}{9}y + 6$

y = _____

6. $3(x + 4) + 6x = 66$

x = _____

7. $7y - 4 = 5y + 14$

y = _____

8. $12m - 6 + 4(3m) = 90$

m = _____

Solving Inequalities: Combined Operations

Solve each inequality.

To solve an inequality with combined operations, solve it as you would solve an equation. Remember to reverse the sign if you multiply or divide by a negative integer.

1. $^-9x \leq 26 + 4x$

2. $2y + 3y < 10$

3. $^-5 + 3y \geq 31$

4. $2(x + 4) > 20$

5. $\dfrac{b}{3} - 6 > 12$

6. $\dfrac{2}{5}a - 4 > 1$

7. $^-2p + 4 < 5p - 10$

8. $3x - 2 < 9x - 4$

More Inequalities

Solve each inequality.

1. $5(y + 2) > 30$

2. $9x - 4x \leq {}^-15$

3. $10 > 5(a + 8)$

4. $30 + 7x > 2$

5. $16p - 4p < 48$

6. $\frac{x}{2} - 2 \geq 10$

7. $7x - 3 \leq {}^-14x + 18$

8. $11m + 9 \geq 5m - 21$

9. $\frac{a}{4} - 7 < {}^-12$

10. ${}^-4(m - 3) > 12$

Graphing on a Number Line

Solve. Graph the solution on a number line.

$$3x + 2 < 5$$
$$3x + 2 - 2 < 5 - 2$$
$$\frac{3x}{3} < \frac{3}{3}$$
$$x < 1$$

$-10\,-9\,-8\,-7\,-6\,-5\,-4\,-3\,-2\,-1\ 0\ 1\ 2\ 3\ 4\ 5\ 6\ 7\ 8\ 9\ 10$

Use a solid circle for $\leq$ or $\geq$.

1. $5x > 10$

$-10\,-9\,-8\,-7\,-6\,-5\,-4\,-3\,-2\,-1\ 0\ 1\ 2\ 3\ 4\ 5\ 6\ 7\ 8\ 9\ 10$

2. $^{-}2x \leq 6$

$-10\,-9\,-8\,-7\,-6\,-5\,-4\,-3\,-2\,-1\ 0\ 1\ 2\ 3\ 4\ 5\ 6\ 7\ 8\ 9\ 10$

3. $2x + 3 \geq 5$

$-10\,-9\,-8\,-7\,-6\,-5\,-4\,-3\,-2\,-1\ 0\ 1\ 2\ 3\ 4\ 5\ 6\ 7\ 8\ 9\ 10$

4. $^{-}3x + 4 \geq ^{-}5$

$-10\,-9\,-8\,-7\,-6\,-5\,-4\,-3\,-2\,-1\ 0\ 1\ 2\ 3\ 4\ 5\ 6\ 7\ 8\ 9\ 10$

5. $2x + 1 < ^{-}7$

$-10\,-9\,-8\,-7\,-6\,-5\,-4\,-3\,-2\,-1\ 0\ 1\ 2\ 3\ 4\ 5\ 6\ 7\ 8\ 9\ 10$

6. $9m + 3 < 6m + 6$

$-10\,-9\,-8\,-7\,-6\,-5\,-4\,-3\,-2\,-1\ 0\ 1\ 2\ 3\ 4\ 5\ 6\ 7\ 8\ 9\ 10$

Graphing on a Coordinate Plane

Graph each point on the coordinate plane.

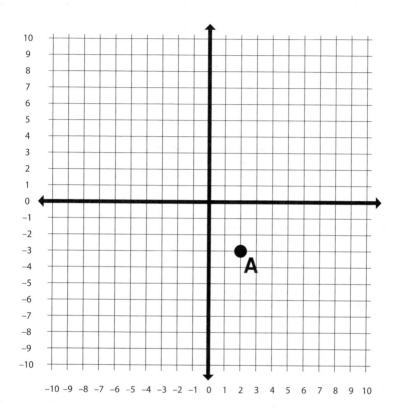

1.   A (2, ‑3)

2.   B (3, 5)

3.   C (‑2, 8)

4.   D (0, 0)

5.   E (‑3, ‑3)

6.   F (‑5, 3)

7.   G (8, 2)

8.   H (5, ‑4)

Graphing Linear Equations

Make a table of solutions, and graph each equation.

$y = 3x + 2$

x	y
-2	-4
-1	-1
0	2
1	5
2	8

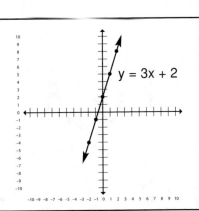

$y = 3x + 2$

1. $y = 3x + 5$

2. $y = 2x - 1$

3. $y = {}^-x + 6$

4. $y = {}^-2x + 3$

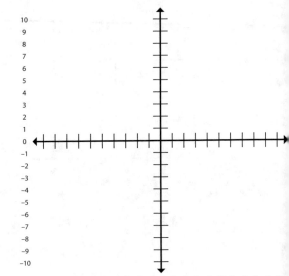

5. $y = 2x - 5$

6. $y = x - 5$

Slope

Find the slope of each line, given two points on that line.

Example:

Slope = $\dfrac{\text{change in y}}{\text{change in x}}$

A(6, ⁻3) and B(⁻2, 3)

$$\dfrac{^-3 - 3}{6 - (^-2)} = \dfrac{^-6}{8} = \dfrac{^-3}{4}$$

1. A(8, 4), B(1, ⁻3)

= _____

2. C(1, 3), D(5, 8)

= _____

3. E(⁻3, 1), F(4, 5)

= _____

4. G(2, 3), H(⁻1, 3)

= _____

5. H(⁻3, 3), I(3, ⁻3)

= _____

6. J(3, 5), K(⁻2, ⁻3)

= _____

7. L($\dfrac{3}{2}$, 1), M($\dfrac{5}{2}$, $\dfrac{1}{2}$)

= _____

8. N(⁻2, 3), O(4, ⁻6)

= _____

Intercepts

Find the x- and y-intercepts.

Example:

x-intercept	y-intercept
Find the value of x when y = 0.	Find the value of y when x = 0.
$y = 2x + 4$	$y = 2x + 4$
$0 = 2x + 4$	$y = 2(0) + 4$
$^-4 = 2x$	$y = \mathbf{4}$
$x = \mathbf{^-2}$	

1. $y = x - 3$

2. $y = {}^-2x - 2$

3. $y = 3x - 4$

4. $y = {}^-5x + 6$

5. $y = \frac{1}{2}x - 5$

6. $y = \frac{1}{3}x - 2$

7. $y = 12 - 6x$

8. $y = 3x - 7$

Graphing Systems of Equations

Use a graph to solve each system of equations.

The point at which two linear equations (a system of equations) intersect is the solution.

$$y = x + 1$$

$$\text{and } y = 2x$$

Solve for x and y. The solution is (1, 2).

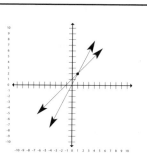

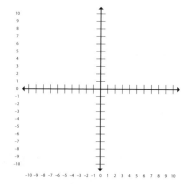

1. $y = 3x + 5$

$y = x + 5$

= _____

2. $y = 4x + 1$

$y = x - 2$

= _____

3. $y = x - 5$

$y = {}^-2x + 4$

= _____

4. $y = 2x + 6$

$y = x + 5$

= _____

Ratio

Write each ratio as a fraction in lowest terms.

1. 16 : 36

= _____

2. 60 to 200

= _____

3. 24 to 60

= _____

4. 7 : 35

= _____

5. 2 violins to 6 cellos

= _____

6. 6 pennies to 12 quarters

= _____

7. 18 : 7

= _____

8. $\frac{16}{28}$

= _____

9. 9 to 24

= _____

10. 45 : 250

= _____

Proportion

Solve for x.

$$\frac{3}{4} = \frac{x}{20}$$

$$3 \cdot 20 = 4 \cdot x$$
$$60 = 4x$$
$$x = \mathbf{15}$$

1. $\frac{1}{2} = \frac{x}{16}$

x = _____

2. $\frac{4}{5} = \frac{x}{65}$

x = _____

3. $\frac{6}{9} = \frac{4}{x}$

x = _____

4. $\frac{8}{12} = \frac{x}{15}$

x = _____

5. $\frac{10}{18} = \frac{x}{27}$

x = _____

6. $\frac{12}{60} = \frac{10}{x}$

x = _____

7. $\frac{100}{x} = \frac{90}{45}$

x = _____

8. $\frac{8}{15} = \frac{x}{45}$

x = _____

9. $\frac{8}{x} = \frac{12}{27}$

x = _____

10. $\frac{4}{9} = \frac{40}{x}$

x = _____

Using Proportions

Use a proportion to solve.

1. Billy is buying soda for a class party. He needs five 2-liter bottles. If three 2-liter bottles cost $7.00, how much will five cost?

_____

2. Angie wants to enlarge a picture. It has a length of 4 inches and a width of 6 inches. If she enlarges the length to 10 inches, how wide will the picture be? _____

3. Marcelle can buy 3 pounds of potatoes for $2.19. How much will 5 pounds cost her?_____

4. If a 10-pound turkey takes 4 hours to cook, how long will it take a 16-pound turkey to cook? _____

5. The ratio of Ratia's height to Janece's height is 5:6. Ratia is 57 inches tall. How tall is Janece?_____

Fractions, Decimals, and Percents

Part I: Express each decimal or fraction as a percent.

Example:

$$0.62 = \textbf{62\%}$$
$$0.62 \times 100 = 62$$

$$\frac{3}{4} = \textbf{75\%}$$
$$3 \div 4 = 0.75 \times 100 = 75$$

1. $0.07 = $ _____

2. $\frac{1}{5} = $ _____

3. $\frac{5}{8} = $ _____

4. $1.13 = $ _____

5. $0.81 = $ _____

6. $\frac{4}{40} = $ _____

Part II: Express each percent as a fraction and a decimal.

Example:

$$56\% = \textbf{0.56} = \frac{14}{25}$$
$$56 \div 100 = 0.56 = \frac{56}{100} = \frac{14}{25}$$

7. $70\% = $ ___,___

8. $35\% = $ ___,___

9. $64\% = $ ___,___

10. $97\% = $ ___,___

11. $0.09\% = $ ___,___

12. $66\frac{2}{3}\% = $ ___,___

More Fractions, Decimals, and Percents

Complete the table.

	Fraction	Decimal	Percent
1.	$\frac{1}{8}$		
2.		0.17	
3.			63%
4.		.53	
5.	$\frac{7}{20}$		
6.			80%
7.		1.25	
8.	$\frac{1}{3}$		

Using Percents

Solve each problem. Round to the nearest percent when necessary.

1. Shakira deposits 15% of her paycheck into her savings account each pay period. If her paycheck is $264, how much should she put into her savings account?_____

2. The Panthers won 8 football games and lost 3. What percentage of their games did they win? _____

3. Hannah answered 39 questions correctly on her science test. There were 42 questions in all. What percentage did she answer correctly? _____

4. Kenny bought a pair of shoes on sale. The sale price was 50% of the original price. He paid with a $50 bill and received $8.75 in change. If there was no tax on the shoes, what was their original price?_____

5. A math test has 60 possible points. What percent correct is 52 points? _____

Angles

Write and solve an equation to find the measure of each angle.

Complementary Angles	Supplementary Angles
Two angles whose sum is 90°	Two angles whose sum is 180°

1. The complement of a 32° angle.

$$x + 32 = 90$$
$$x + 32 - 32 = 90 - 32$$
$$x = \mathbf{58}$$

2. The supplement of a 105° angle. _____

3. The supplement of a 63° angle. _____

4. The complement of a 13° angle. _____

5. The supplement of a 139° angle. _____

6. The complement of a 45° angle. _____

7. The complement of a 27° angle. _____

8. The supplement of a right angle. _____

Triangles

Write and solve an equation to find the value of *x*.

The sum of the measures of the angles of a triangle equals 180°.

1.

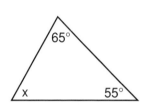

X = _____

2.

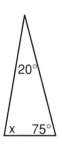

X = _____

3.

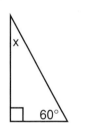

X = _____

4.

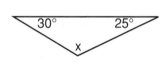

X = _____

5.

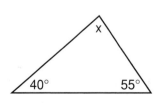

X = _____

6.

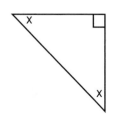

X = _____

Circles and Circumference

Find the circumference of each circle with the given radius or diameter. Use 3.14 for π.

Circumference is the distance around a circle.
C = πd or 2πr

1. d = 8 cm

C = __**25.12 cm**__

2. r = 5 cm

C = _____

3. r = 18 cm

C = _____

4. d = 10 m

C = _____

5. r = 2.5 cm

C = _____

6. d = 3.2 m

C = _____

7. d = 6.1 cm

C = _____

8. r = 10 cm

C = _____

9. r = 12.9 cm

C = _____

10. d = 11 m

C = _____

Area of Rectangles and Parallelograms

Part I: Find the area of each rectangle.

Area = length • width
A = lw

1.

22 cm

12 cm

2.

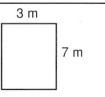

3 m

7 m

A = **22•12 = 264 cm²**

A = _____

3.

14.5 m

9.2 m

4.

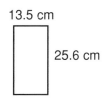

13.5 cm

25.6 cm

A = _____

A = _____

Part II: Find the area of each parallelogram.

Area = base • height
A = bh

5.

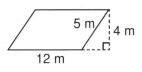

5 m

4 m

12 m

6.

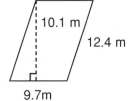

10.1 m

12.4 m

9.7m

A = _____

A = _____

7.

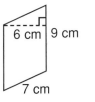

6 cm | 9 cm

7 cm

8.

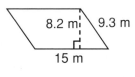

8.2 m | 9.3 m

15 m

A = _____

A = _____

Area of Triangles and Trapezoids

Part I: Find the area of each triangle.

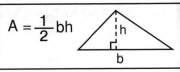

$A = \dfrac{1}{2}bh$

1.

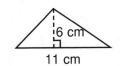

6 cm

11 cm

A = _____

2.

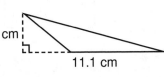

7.2 cm

11.1 cm

A = _____

3.

4 m   5 m

3 m

A = _____

4.

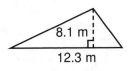

8.1 m

12.3 m

A = _____

Part II: Find the area of each trapezoid.

$A = \dfrac{1}{2}h(b_1 + b_2)$

b_1

h

b_2

5.

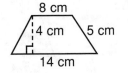

8 cm

4 cm   5 cm

14 cm

A = _____

6.

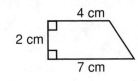

4 cm

2 cm

7 cm

A = _____

7.

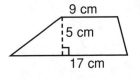

9 cm

5 cm

17 cm

A = _____

8.

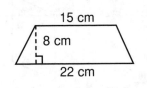

15 cm

8 cm

22 cm

A = _____

Area of Circles

Find the area of each circle with the given radius or diameter. Use 3.14 for π. Round to the nearest hundredth.

Example:

$$A = \pi r^2$$

$r = 3$ cm
$A = 3.14 \cdot 3^2$
$A = \mathbf{28.26}$ **cm**^{2}

1. $d = 10$ cm

$A =$ _____

2. $r = 4.9$ m

$A =$ _____

3. $r = 60$ cm

$A =$ _____

4. $d = 4.8$ m

$A =$ _____

5. $d = 8$ cm

$A =$ _____

6. $r = 150$ cm

$A =$ _____

7. $d = 17.8$ cm

$A =$ _____

8. $r = 14.2$ m

$A =$ _____

9. $r = 32$ cm

$A =$ _____

10. $d = 21$ cm

$A =$ _____

Volume of Prisms

Find the volume of each prism.

V = Bh, where B = *area of the base* and h = *height of the prism* Write your answer in cubic units.

1.

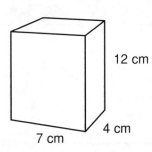

12 cm

4 cm

7 cm

V = **(7 • 4) • 12 = 336** cm³

2.

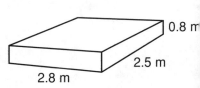

0.8 m

2.5 m

2.8 m

V = _____

3.

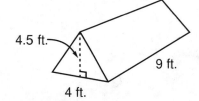

4.5 ft.

9 ft.

4 ft.

V = _____

4.

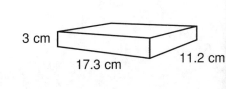

3 cm

17.3 cm

11.2 cm

V = _____

5.

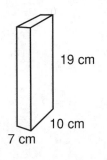

19 cm

10 cm

7 cm

V = _____

6.

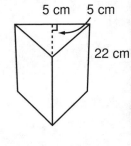

5 cm 5 cm

22 cm

V = _____

Volume of Cylinders

Find the volume of each cylinder. Use 3.14 for π. Round to the nearest hundredth.

$V = \pi r^2 h$, where h = height of the cylinder
Write your answer in cubic units.

1.

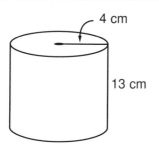

4 cm

13 cm

V = _____

2.

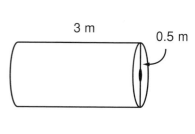

3 m

0.5 m

V = _____

3.

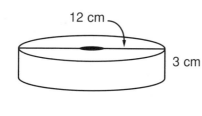

12 cm

3 cm

V = _____

4.

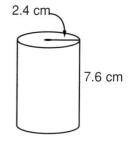

2.4 cm

7.6 cm

V = _____

5.

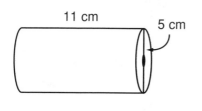

11 cm

5 cm

V = _____

6.

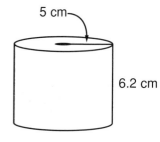

5 cm

6.2 cm

V = _____

Surface Area

Find the surface area of the prisms or cylinders. When needed, use the Pythagorean theorem, and use 3.14 for π.

To find the surface area of a prism or cylinder, find the area of each surface; then add them all together.

1.

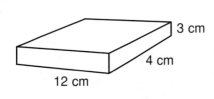

3 cm

4 cm

12 cm

= _____

2.

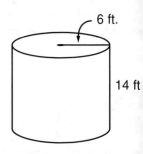

6 ft.

14 ft

= _____

3.

4.5 cm

3.6 cm   9.1 cm

= _____

4.

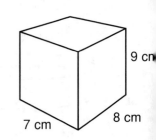

9 cm

7 cm   8 cm

= _____

5.

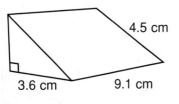

12 in.

5 in.

= _____

6.

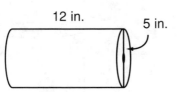

4 cm

26 cm

26 cm

= _____

Square Roots

Find each square root.

1. $\sqrt{81}$

= _____

2. $\sqrt{9}$

= _____

3. $\sqrt{64}$

= _____

4. $\sqrt{36}$

= _____

5. $\sqrt{16}$

= _____

6. $\sqrt{121}$

= _____

7. $\sqrt{100}$

= _____

8. $\sqrt{144}$

= _____

9. $\sqrt{169}$

= _____

10. $\sqrt{400}$

= _____

Solving Equations Using Square Roots

Solve each equation.

Example:

$$x^2 = 16$$
$$\sqrt{x^2} = \sqrt{16}$$

x = **4** or **⁻4**, which you can write (**±4**).

1. $x^2 = 25$

X = _____

2. $x^2 = 4$

X = _____

3. $x^2 = 36$

X = _____

4. $x^2 = 49$

X = _____

5. $x^2 = 100$

X = _____

6. $x^2 = 81$

X = _____

7. $x^2 = 121$

X = _____

8. $x^2 = 1$

X = _____

9. $x^2 = 196$

X = _____

10. $x^2 = 256$

X = _____

The Pythagorean Theorem

Use the Pythagorean theorem to find the missing length *a*, *b*, or *c*. Round decimal answers to the nearest tenth.

The Pythagorean theorem

$$a^2 + b^2 = c^2$$

a   c

b

Find c if a = 3 and b = 4.

$$3^2 + 4^2 = c^2$$

$$9 + 16 = c^2$$

$$25 = c^2$$

$$c = \textbf{5}$$

1. Find c if a = 9 and b = 40.

c = _____

2. Find c if a = 24 and b = 7.

c = _____

3. Find a if b = 5 and c = 13.

a = _____

4. Find b if a = 30 and c = 34.

b = _____

5. Find b if a = 9 and c = 15.

b = _____

6. Find a if b = 8 and c = 20.

a = _____

Using the Pythagorean Theorem

Use the Pythagorean theorem ($a^2 + b^2 = c^2$) to solve each problem. Draw a picture if necessary. Round answers to the nearest tenth.

1. The base of a 30-foot ladder is 8 feet from the building it is leaning against. How high above the ground is the ladder? _____

2. A television measures 10 inches long. It has a diagonal measure across the screen of 12 inches. How tall is the television screen?_____

3. The diagonal brace on a tree is 5 feet long. The brace hits the tree at 4 feet off the ground. How far is the end of the brace from the base of the tree? _____

4. Janet and her friends go on a hike. They hike 7 miles east, then 3 miles south to find the waterfall. How far are they from their starting point?_____

5. Raoul takes a shortcut to school. He walks diagonally through a parking lot that measures 20 meters wide by 40 meters long. How much shorter is the shortcut than a route walking along the sides of the lot? _____

Solve Problems by Using an Equation

Write and solve an equation to find the solution.

1. The setting of a movie takes place 17 years before the year 1995. In what year is the movie set? _____

2. A theater sold $8,125 worth of tickets. If each ticket cost $6.50, how many tickets did the theater sell? _____

3. Catherine paid $22 for a sweater on sale. It was reduced by $13. What was the original price? _____

4. Last season Carlos scored 5 more runs than twice the number he batted in. He scored 123 runs last season. How many runs did Carlos bat in? _____

5. Jana needs to take a taxi home. When the meter in the taxi is first turned on, it reads $2.20. As the taxi travels, $1.50 is added for each mile driven. Her final fare is $12.70. How many miles was her trip? _____

6. Mike scored 10 points less than twice the lowest score on a science test. If his score was 96, what was the lowest score on the test? _____

Solve Problems by Using Logical Reasoning

Solve each problem.

1. Marissa, Kim, John, and Rusty live in the towns Jamestown, Redan, Monroe, and Klarksville. None of them live in a town that has the same first letter as their first name. Marissa has spent all of her life in Klarksville. Neither John nor Rusty has ever been to Monroe. Which person lives in which town?

_____

2. Dave and his friends are sitting at a large round table playing a game. Dave's mom baked some cookies for them. She passed around a tray of 25 cookies. Each person took one cookie at a time until there were no more cookies left. Dave took the first cookie and the last cookie, and he may have taken more than that. How many people could have been sitting at the table?_____

3. Two men and two women each play a different musical instrument. The players' names are Steve, Julius, Jody, and Nancy. One plays the violin, one plays the flute, one plays the drums, and one plays the piano. Nancy's brother is part of this group; he plays the drums and is married to the one who plays the violin. The one who plays piano doesn't have any brothers or sisters. Both Julius and the one who plays the flute are single. Who plays which instrument?_____

4. The varsity basketball team won 3 out of every 4 games it played this year. It lost 12 games. How many did it win?

_____

Solve Problems by Working Backwards

Solve each problem by working backwards.

1. A certain number is multiplied by 5, and then 9 is added to the result. The final answer is 44. What is the number?

_____

2. A certain number is divided by 5, and then 2 is subtracted from the result. The final answer is 29. What is the number?

_____

3. Janie is at basketball practice. She stretches for 8 minutes; then she does 3 minutes of push-ups and 4 minutes of jumping jacks. Finally, she runs for 22 minutes. If Janie finishes running at 4:07 p.m., when did she start stretching?

_____

4. Jalen was assigned some math problems for homework. He did half of the problems in class. While waiting for the bus, he did 5 more problems. If he still has 11 problems left, how many problems did his teacher assign?

_____

5. Marley had some goldfish. She gave half of them to Beth. Beth then gave a third of her goldfish to Barry. Barry gave a fourth of his goldfish to Mark. If Mark has 9 goldfish, how many goldfish did Marley have in the beginning? _____

Solve Problems Using Integers

Solve each problem.

1. Jerry's final score on the game he was playing was 70. Midway through the game, his score was ⁻25. How many points did he score during the last half of the game? _____

2. Suppose you are multiplying 3 or more integers. Write a rule that will help you determine the sign of the products.

_____

3. Josh and Susie get on the elevator at the 1st floor. Josh gets off at the 12th floor, and Susie gets off 10 floors above that. Regan gets on the elevator when Susie gets off. If Regan goes down 8 floors, and then gets off, what floor is she on?

_____

4. The product of two integers is ⁻56. One of the integers is 8. What is the other one? _____

5. If a diver descends at a rate of 4 meters per minute, at what depth will she be after 8 minutes? _____

6. The net change in the price of a stock over a one-year period was ⁻$126. What was the average change per month?

_____

Find the Equation

Complete the table below by filling in the missing numbers. Then answer the following questions based on the table.

1.

First Number	-2	-1	0	1	2	3	4	5	10	-10
Second Number	-11	-8	-5	-2	1					

2. What pattern do you notice in the second numbers?

_____

3. How are the second numbers related to the first numbers?

_____

4. If y is the second number and x is the first number, write an equation that represents the relationship between x and y.

_____

Area and Perimeter of Irregular Shapes

Find the area and perimeter of each figure. All angles are right angles.

1.

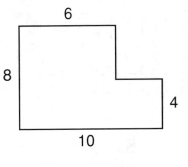

p = _____

a = _____

2.

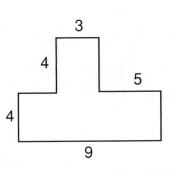

p = _____

a = _____

3.

p = _____

a = _____

4.

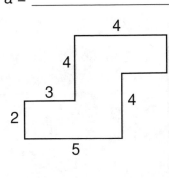

p = _____

a = _____

Comparing Slopes

Solve each problem.

1. Consider the graphs of $y = 2x$, $y = {}^-2x$, and $y = \frac{1}{2}x$.

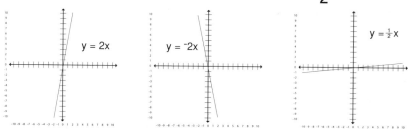

a. Describe each graph. _____

_____

_____

b. How is the graph of $y = 2x$ similar to $y = {}^-2x$? How are

they different? _____

c. How is the graph of $y = 2x$ similar to $y = \frac{1}{2}x$? How are

they different? _____

2. Use a table of solutions to graph the following linear

equations: $y = 3x$, $y = 3x + 1$, $y = 3x + 2$, $y = 3x + 3$.

a. How are the graphs similar? _____

b. How are they different? _____

Interpreting Graphs

Use the line graph below to answer each question.

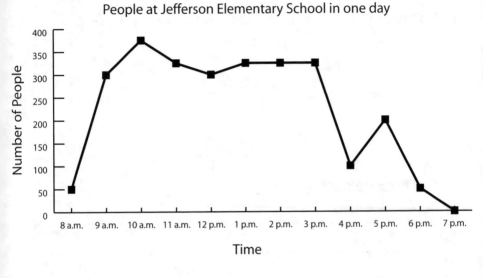

People at Jefferson Elementary School in one day

1. Why did the number of people go up so drastically between 8:00 and 9:00 a.m.? _____

2. How many people were in the building at 1:00 p.m.? _____

3. Approximately how many students attend Jefferson Elementary School? _____

4. How many more people were in the building at 5:00 p.m. than 4:00 p.m.? _____

5. Why do you suppose there were so many people in the building at 5:00 p.m.? _____

6. Describe the point at 7:00 p.m. _____

Answer Pages

Page 1
1. 2^3
2. 10^6
3. y^4
4. m^7
5. 729
6. 2,401
7. 25
8. 100,000,000
9. 64
10. 64

Page 2
1. 3
2. 11
3. 33
4. 63
5. 22
6. 15
7. 40
8. 36
9. 2
10. 3

Page 3
1. 36
2. 5
3. 6
4. 9
5. 9
6. 0
7. 66
8. 6
9. 37
10. 21

Page 4
1. $n = 56$
2. $x = 177$
3. $y = 135$
4. $b = 142$
5. $p = 242$
6. $r = 324$
7. $x = 277$
8. $a = 771$

Page 5
1. $x = 60$
2. $b = 146$
3. $w = 64$
4. $y = 496$
5. $k = 108$
6. $r = 510$
7. $x = 417$
8. $p = 31$
9. $x = 192$
10. $m = 111$

Page 6
1. $y = 49$
2. $x = 24$
3. $b = 132$
4. $x = 207$
5. $y = 528$
6. $m = 36$
7. $a = 12$
8. $m = 3,948$

Page 7
1. $m = 23$
2. $x = 518$
3. $a = 25$
4. $k = 12$
5. $b = 1,616$
6. $r = 720$
7. $p = 27$
8. $x = 594$
9. $w = 18$
10. $n = 496$

Page 8
1. 9
2. 0
3. ⁻8
4. 4
5. ⁻2
6. 2
7. 8
8. 5
9. 12
10. 21
11. 83
12. 100
13. 142
14. 231
15. 250

Page 9
1. <
2. >
3. >
4. =
5. >
6. <
7. ⁻4, ⁻2, 5
8. ⁻10, ⁻7, ⁻3, ⁻2
9. ⁻14, 5, 12, |⁻17|
10. ⁻3, ⁻2, |⁻4|, |5|

Page 10
1. ⁻10
2. ⁻15
3. 16
4. ⁻12
5. 34
6. ⁻24

Page 11
1. ⁻6
2. ⁻17
3. 18
4. 7
5. ⁻6
6. 44
7. 16
8. ⁻9
9. ⁻148
10. 14
11. ⁻14
12. 0

Page 12
1. $c = 5$
2. $a = ⁻117$
3. $b = ⁻168$
4. $y = 0$
5. $p = 67$
6. $x = ⁻122$
7. $y = 37$
8. $r = ⁻279$
9. $y = ⁻220$
10. $c = ⁻117$

Answer Pages

Page 13
1. ⁻45   2. 42   3. ⁻21   4. 30
5. 30   6. ⁻81   7. 0   8. ⁻72
9. ⁻144   10. 460   11. ⁻40   12. 96

Page 14
1. 4   2. 9   3. ⁻6   4. ⁻6
5. 0   6. ⁻7   7. ⁻25   8. ⁻8
9. 9   10. ⁻18   11. 5   12. ⁻13

Page 15
1. $x = ⁻43$ 2. $y = ⁻28$
3. $b = ⁻182$ 4. $x = ⁻396$
5. $c = 34$ 6. $n = ⁻15$
7. $x = ⁻45$ 8. $m = 32$
9. $y = 2,120$ 10. $x = ⁻688$

Page 16
1. $m > ⁻5$ 2. $y < 17$
3. $p \le 6$ 4. $m \ge -50$
5. $y > 37$ 6. $m \le 8$
7. $p \ge ⁻24$ 8. $x \ge 39$

Page 17
1. $m < ⁻168$ 2. $n \ge ⁻17$
3. $y > ⁻11$ 4. $x \le ⁻63$
5. $n > 5$ 6. $x < ⁻4$
7. $n \le 6$ 8. $w < 84$

Page 18
1. 68.7   2. 67.8   3. 70.1   4. 3.402
5. 9.74   6. 6.69   7. 100.62   8. 5.25

Page 19
1. $y = 5.38$ 2. $y = 1.7$
3. $p = -3.843$ 4. $x = 9.14$
5. $m = -38.13$ 6. $a = 1.67$
7. $b = 64.45$ 8. $w = 26.29$

Page 20
1. 0.198   2. ⁻1.6566
3. 3.35   4. ⁻0.4304
5. ⁻52.8   6. 31.0996
7. ⁻803.88   8. ⁻7,520

Page 21
1. ⁻0.023   2. 0.0798
3. 27   4. ⁻2,190
5. ⁻520   6. 0.0025
7. 0.045   8. ⁻15.3

Page 22
1. $y = ⁻1.6$ 2. $m = ⁻15$
3. $p = 1.092$ 4. $x = ⁻17.28$
5. $y = 20$ 6. $r = ⁻12$
7. $x = ⁻0.11$ 8. $m = ⁻5.976$

Page 23
1. $\frac{3}{5}$ 2. $\frac{7}{12}$ 3. $\frac{2}{3}$ 4. $\frac{3}{5}$
5. $\frac{7}{9}$ 6. $\frac{8}{11}$ 7. $\frac{39}{56}$ 8. $\frac{1}{4}$
9. $\frac{5}{6}$ 10. $\frac{11}{17}$ 11. $\frac{5a}{16}$ 12. $\frac{a}{2}$

Page 24
1. $4\frac{1}{6}$ 2. 18   3. $33\frac{4}{5}$ 4. $6\frac{4}{7}$
5. $6\frac{1}{4}$ 6. 5   7. $\frac{41}{16}$ 8. $\frac{73}{11}$
9. $\frac{83}{10}$ 10. $\frac{109}{10}$ 11. $\frac{253}{50}$ 12. $\frac{167}{8}$

Page 25
1. >   2. >   3. <   4. >
5. $\frac{2}{5}, \frac{2}{4}, \frac{2}{3}$ 6. $\frac{3}{8}, \frac{6}{7}, \frac{7}{8}$ 7. $\frac{⁻7}{8}, \frac{⁻3}{4}, \frac{⁻5}{9}$ 8. $\frac{⁻2}{3}, \frac{⁻6}{15}, \frac{⁻5}{13}$

Page 26
1. $\frac{6}{13}$ 2. $\frac{7}{11}$ 3. $\frac{⁻2}{9}$ 4. $\frac{1}{7}$
5. $\frac{11}{15}$ 6. $\frac{⁻1}{8}$ 7. 0   8. $⁻2\frac{5}{7}$

Answer Pages

Page 27
1. $1\frac{2}{25}$ **2.** $\frac{1}{12}$ **3.** $\frac{11}{20}$ **4.** $1\frac{8}{15}$
5. $\frac{5}{28}$ **6.** $^{-}1\frac{3}{20}$ **7.** $\frac{7}{9}$ **8.** $\frac{1}{10}$

Page 28
1. $12\frac{1}{12}$ **2.** $\frac{3}{4}$ **3.** $3\frac{9}{20}$ **4.** $^{-}6\frac{4}{7}$
5. $2\frac{14}{15}$ **6.** $6\frac{43}{45}$ **7.** 3 **8.** 1

Page 29
1. $x = 1\frac{1}{9}$ **2.** $a = ^{-}5\frac{1}{3}$
3. $m = 2\frac{1}{8}$ **4.** $x = 5\frac{1}{2}$
5. $b = \frac{^{-}1}{4}$ **6.** $n = \frac{8}{15}$
7. $x = \frac{13}{50}$ **8.** $y = ^{-}1\frac{103}{240}$

Page 30
1. $\frac{7}{16}$ **2.** $\frac{^{-}1}{3}$ **3.** $^{-}20$ **4.** $^{-}3$
5. 4 **6.** $^{-}12\frac{8}{9}$ **7.** $6\frac{7}{8}$ **8.** $43\frac{1}{5}$

Page 31
1. $\frac{5}{7}$ **2.** $\frac{9}{10}$ **3.** $\frac{^{-}3}{40}$ **4.** $^{-}4$
5. $1\frac{5}{16}$ **6.** $\frac{^{-}91}{135}$ **7.** $^{-}\frac{25}{41}$ **8.** $-1\frac{3}{7}$

Page 32
1. $m = \frac{1}{16}$ **2.** $x = 5\frac{3}{5}$
3. $x = ^{-}1\frac{2}{5}$ **4.** $x = \frac{18}{25}$
5. $p = ^{-}1\frac{1}{9}$ **6.** $y = 6\frac{2}{5}$
7. $y = ^{-}1\frac{17}{23}$ **8.** $x = 27\frac{3}{5}$

Page 33
1. 2 **2.** 9^4 **3.** $(^{-}3)^2$ **4.** 5
5. m^2 **6.** x^5 **7.** $(^{-}4)^3$ **8.** y^3

Page 34
1. $y = 9$ **2.** $x = 5$
3. $p = 5$ **4.** $c = 4.75$
5. $m = ^{-}28$ **6.** $x = 24$
7. $y = 14$ **8.** $p = ^{-}14$

Page 35
1. $x = 4$ **2.** $p = 3$
3. $y = ^{-}6$ **4.** $m = 12$
5. $a = ^{-}3$ **6.** $y = ^{-}3$
7. $x = 2$ **8.** $y = 5$

Page 36
1. $c = 2$ **2.** $x = ^{-}4$
3. $p = 63$ **4.** $a = 10$

Page 37
1. $x = 2$ **2.** $y = 2$
3. $a = 72$ **4.** $p = ^{-}5$
5. $y = 18$ **6.** $x = 6$
7. $y = 9$ **8.** $m = 4$

Page 38
1. $x \geq ^{-}2$ **2.** $y < 2$ **3.** $y \geq 12$ **4.** $x > 6$
5. $b > 54$ **6.** $a > 12\frac{1}{2}$ **7.** $p > 2$ **8.** $x > \frac{1}{3}$

Page 39
1. $y > 4$ **2.** $x \leq ^{-}3$
3. $a < ^{-}6$ **4.** $x > ^{-}4$
5. $p < 4$ **6.** $x \geq 24$
7. $x \leq 1$ **8.** $m \geq ^{-}5$
9. $a < ^{-}20$ **10.** $m < 0$

Page 40
1. $x > 2$, **2.** $x \geq ^{-}3$,
3. $x \geq 1$, **4.** $x \leq 3$,
5. $x < ^{-}4$, **6.** $m < 1$,

Answer Pages

Page 41

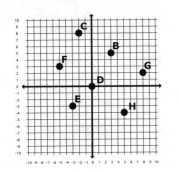

Page 42

1.

x	y
0	5
⁻1	2
⁻2	⁻1

2.

x	y
⁻2	⁻5
⁻1	⁻3
0	⁻1
1	1

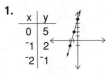

3.

x	y
0	6
1	5
2	4

4.

x	y
0	3
1	1

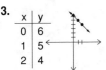

5.

x	y
0	⁻5
1	⁻3
2	⁻1

6.

x	y
0	⁻5
1	⁻4
2	⁻3

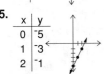

Page 43

1. 1   **2.** $\frac{5}{4}$ **3.** $\frac{4}{7}$ **4.** 0

5. ⁻1   **6.** $\frac{8}{5}$ **7.** $\frac{-1}{2}$ **8.** $\frac{-3}{2}$

Page 44

1. x = 3, y = ⁻3   **2.** x = ⁻1, y = ⁻2

3. x = $\frac{4}{3}$, y = ⁻4   **4.** x = $\frac{6}{5}$, y = 6

5. x = 10, y = ⁻5   **6.** x = 6, y = ⁻2

7. x = 2, y = 12   **8.** x = $\frac{7}{3}$, y = ⁻7

Page 45

1. (0, 5)   **2.** (⁻1, ⁻3)   **3.** (3, ⁻2)   **4.** (⁻1, 4)

Page 46

1. $\frac{4}{9}$ **2.** $\frac{3}{10}$ **3.** $\frac{2}{5}$ **4.** $\frac{1}{5}$

5. $\frac{1}{3}$ **6.** $\frac{1}{2}$ **7.** $\frac{18}{7}$ **8.** $\frac{4}{7}$

9. $\frac{3}{8}$ **10.** $\frac{9}{50}$

Page 47

1. 8   **2.** 52   **3.** 6   **4.** 10

5. 15   **6.** 50   **7.** 50   **8.** 24

9. 18   **10.** 90

Page 48

1. $11.67   **2.** 15 inches

3. $3.65

4. 6 hours, 24 minutes

5. 68.4 inches

Page 49

1. 7%   **2.** 20%   **3.** 62.5%

4. 113%   **5.** 81%   **6.** 10%

7. .7, $\frac{7}{10}$ **8.** .35, $\frac{7}{20}$ **9.** .64, $\frac{16}{25}$

10. .97, $\frac{97}{100}$ **11.** .0009, $\frac{9}{10000}$ **12.** .67, $\frac{2}{3}$

Page 50

1. 0.125, 12.5%   **2.** $\frac{17}{100}$, 17%

3. $\frac{63}{100}$, 0.63   **4.** $\frac{53}{100}$, 53%

5. 0.35, 35%   **6.** $\frac{4}{5}$, 0.8

7. $1\frac{1}{4}$, 125%   **8.** 0.33, $33\frac{1}{3}$%

Page 51

1. $39.60   **2.** 73%   **3.** 93%

4. $82.50   **5.** 87%

Page 52

1. 58°   **2.** 75°   **3.** 117°   **4.** 77°

5. 41°   **6.** 45°   **7.** 63°   **8.** 90°

Page 53

1. x = 60°   **2.** x = 85°

3. x = 30°   **4.** x = 125°

5. x = 85°   **6.** x = 45°

Answer Pages

Page 54
1. 25.12 cm
2. 31.4 cm
3. 113.04 cm
4. 31.4 m
5. 15.7 cm
6. 10.048 m
7. 19.154 cm
8. 62.8 cm
9. 81.012 cm
10. 34.54 m

Page 55
1. 264 cm^2
2. 21 m^2
3. 133.4 m^2
4. 345.6 cm^2
5. 48 m^2
6. 97.97 m^2
7. 54 cm^2
8. 123 m^2

Page 56
1. 33 cm^2
2. 39.96 cm^2
3. 6 m^2
4. 49.815 m^2
5. 44 cm^2
6. 11 cm^2
7. 65 cm^2
8. 148 cm^2

Page 57
1. 78.5 cm^2
2. 75.39 m^2
3. 11,304 cm^2
4. 18.09 m^2
5. 50.24 cm^2
6. 70,650 cm^2
7. 248.72 cm^2
8. 633.15 m^2
9. 3,215.36 cm^2
10. 346.19 cm^2

Page 58
1. 336 cm^3
2. 5.6 m^3
3. 81 ft.^{3}
4. 581.28 cm^3
5. 1,330 cm^3
6. 275 cm^3

Page 59
1. 653.12 cm^3
2. 0.59 m^3
3. 339.12 cm^3
4. 137.46 cm^3
5. 215.88 cm^3
6. 486.7 cm^3

Page 60
1. 192 cm^2
2. 753.6 ft.^{2}
3. 108 cm^2
4. 382 cm^2
5. 227.65 in.^{2}
6. 1,768 cm^2

Page 61
1. 9
2. 3
3. 8
4. 6
5. 4
6. 11
7. 10
8. 12
9. 13
10. 20

Page 62
1. $x = \pm 5$
2. $x = \pm 2$
3. $x = \pm 6$
4. $x = \pm 7$
5. $x = \pm 10$
6. $x = \pm 9$
7. $x = \pm 11$
8. $x = \pm 1$
9. $x = \pm 14$
10. $x = \pm 16$

Page 63
1. $c = 41$
2. $c = 25$
3. $a = 12$
4. $b = 16$
5. $b = 12$
6. $a = 18.3$

Page 64
1. 28.9 ft.
2. 6.6 in.
3. 3 ft.
4. 7.6 miles
5. 15.3 m

Page 65
1. $x + 17 = 1995$; $x = 1978$
2. $(8125) \div x = 6.5$; $x = 1,250$ tickets
3. $x - 13 = 22$; $x = \$35$
4. $2b + 5 = 123$; $b = 59$
5. $2.20 + 1.50x = 12.70$; $x = 7$ miles
6. $2t - 10 = 96$; $t = 53$

Page 66
1. Marissa – Klarksville; Kim – Monroe; John – Redan; Rusty – Jamestown
2. 3, 4, 6, 8, 12, or 24 people
3. Steve – drums; Jody – violin; Nancy – flute; Julius – piano
4. 36 games

Page 67
1. 7
2. 155
3. 3:30 p.m.
4. 32 problems
5. 216 goldfish

Answer Pages

Page 68
1. 95 points
2. An even number of negative integers will give a positive product. An odd number of negative integers will give a negative product.
3. 14th floor
4. $^-7$
5. $^-32$ m
6. $^-$\$10.50

Page 69
1. 4, 7, 10, 25, $^-35$
2. They increase by 3 as the first number increases by 1.
3. Multiply the first number by 3 and then subtract 5.
4. $y = 3x - 5$

Page 70
1. $A = 64$ u^2; $P = 36$ u
2. $A = 48$ u^2; $P = 34$ u
3. $A = 42$ u^2; $P = 30$ u
4. $A = 22$ u^2; $P = 26$ u

Page 71
1. **a.** $y = 2x$; positive, steep slope
   $y = ^-2x$; negative, steep slope
   $y = \frac{1}{2}x$; positive, less steep slope
   b. Similar: Both are steep. Different: One is a positive slope; the other is a negative slope.
   c. Similar: Both are positive slopes. Different: One is more steep than the other.
2. **a.** They all have the same slopes.
   b. They all have different intercepts.

Page 72
1. The students were arriving at school for the beginning of the day.
2. approximately 325
3. about 300
4. 100 people
5. Answers may vary. Sample answer: Possibly because there was an after-school program that brought in parents.
6. Everyone has left the building for the day.